Words that are tricky to understand are in **bold**. Find out what they mean in the glossary.

Words that are difficult to say are in *italics*. Find out how to say them at the back of the book.

COULD WE SURVIVE WITHOUT SEAWEED?

DISCOVER THE SCIENCE BEHIND ***PHYCOLOGY***
(fy-KOH-luh-jee)

Written by Rosie Rowntree
Illustrated by Denis Alonso

WHAT IS PHYCOLOGY?

Phycology is the study of seaweed. It includes studying how and where seaweed grows, and how important it is to life on Earth – both in the water and on dry land.

The scientists who study seaweed are called **PHYCOLOGISTS.**

When you find seaweed in a rock pool or washed up on a beach, it may not look like much. But appearances can be deceiving!

Seaweed plays an important role in nature and its **ecosystems,** and is helping to protect our planet!

Seaweed is a type of **algae** that grows at the edges of the oceans. Scientists called *phycologists*, who study seaweed, believe there are over 12,000 different kinds! They sort seaweed into three main categories: red, green, and brown.

Kelp is a very big kind of brown seaweed. It can grow as much in one day as some trees on land grow in a whole year!

Kelp grows in large groups called "kelp forests". They're like **underwater cities!**

Kelp forests are important **habitats.** On the surface of the water, sea otters wrap themselves in strands of kelp to avoid drifting away while they sleep.

Phycologists have spotted large animals like whales using kelp forests to hide from **predators**!

Many smaller animals including seals, sea stars, and sea anemones also call kelp forests home!

Animals don't just use seaweed as shelter. There are plenty of creatures – like crabs and lobsters – who prefer to eat it instead! This makes seaweed an important part of the **food chain.**

If seaweed disappeared, many creatures around the world would struggle to survive.

Seaweed doesn't just provide food and shelter. It can also help to protect the oceans from **pollution**.

If **chemicals** used on land get washed into the ocean, they can harm the ecosystem. Helpfully, seaweed can soak these chemicals up like a sponge and **keep the water clean!**

Seaweed can also defend the **coastline** from **erosion**! When a lot of seaweed grows in one place, it **shields** nearby land from big, powerful waves and stops it from getting worn away.

It's not just animals that find seaweed tasty. Humans do too! It has lots of nutrients in it which can help **keep us healthy.**

It can be used as an ingredient in things like pasta, sushi, and even popcorn!

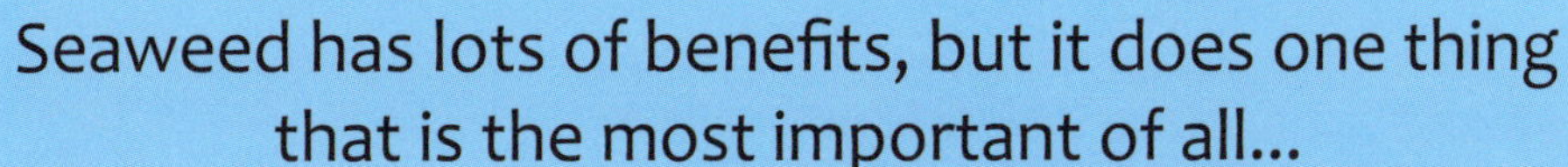

Seaweed has lots of benefits, but it does one thing that is the most important of all...

It gets energy from sunlight through **photosynthesis**. As part of this process, **oxygen** is released. In fact, seaweed and other sea **species** help to produce

most of the oxygen that we breathe!

Unfortunately, some human activity can cause a lot of damage to seaweed. Large fishing boats called trawlers drag huge nets across the bottom of the sea. This can rip certain kinds of seaweed – particularly kelp – from the seabed.

Even small boats simply dropping their anchors can have a negative effect.

Seaweed is also facing challenges because of **climate change**, which is causing our planet to get hotter and hotter. Seaweed might struggle to grow if the oceans get too warm, leaving only the **stipes** behind.

Less seaweed would see many animals lose their habitats and food. Our coastlines would be at risk of more erosion. And we would lose a very important source of oxygen!

Despite these threats, phycologists believe seaweed could actually play a role in tackling climate change.

They are looking into whether seaweed could be grown to help soak up a **greenhouse gas** called **carbon dioxide,** stopping it from harming the planet. There's a lot of research that still needs to be done – but scientists are hopeful!

Despite its simple existence at the bottom of the food chain, humans and animals rely on seaweed for shelter, food, and oxygen to breathe.

And scientists believe it could be used as a tool to help protect the **environment** – and therefore us. Seaweed is nature's unsung hero and we couldn't live without it!

Record-breaking

SEAWEED

There are thousands of diferent kinds of seaweed. It can be found all across the world. Here are some record-breaking seaweed!

BIGGEST KELP FOREST

One of the world's biggest kelp forests is found in the Great Southern Reef off the coast of Australia. The reef is four times bigger than the Great Barrier Reef, and has more types of seaweed than anywhere else on Earth!

LARGEST TYPE OF SEAWEED

The largest type of seaweed in the world is giant kelp. It usually grows up to 100 feet (30 m) long. But in ideal conditions it can grow up to 175 feet (53 m). That's as long as two blue whales!

EARLIEST SEAWEED

Scientists have discovered that the earliest relatives of modern-day seaweed first appeared on Earth over 1.6 billion years ago. That's 1.3 billion years before the dinosaurs first appeared!

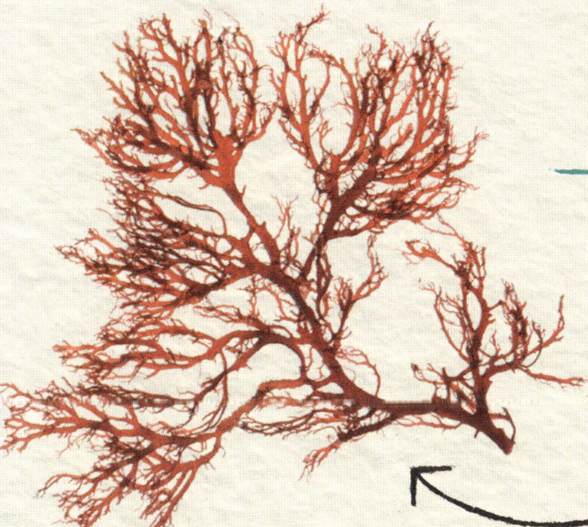

MOST COMMON SEAWEED

There are more types of red seaweed than green or brown. Phycologists think there are over 6,000 different types of red seaweed! This includes some of the most popular seaweed eaten by humans.

BIGGEST SEAWEED PRODUCERS

Six countries in Asia are responsible for growing most of the world's farmed seaweed. But more countries worldwide are now learning about seaweed's benefits and setting up their own seaweed farms.

Super

SEAWEED FACTS

There's so much to discover about the world of phycology. Did you know these incredible facts about seaweed?

RED SEAWEED CAN HELP PRODUCE LESS METHANE!

Red seaweed can be used in food for cows to help them produce less methane. Methane is a greenhouse gas, so reducing the amount that is produced is better for the environment.

SEAWEED IS VERY HEALTHY!

People have been eating seaweed for thousands and thousands of years. It is likely that eating seaweed was actually more common a long time ago than it is now!

ANIMALS USE SEAWEED FOR DISGUISE!

The *Halimeda* ghost pipefish looks a lot like a piece of seaweed! It uses this to its advantage, blending in with its surroundings to avoid larger animals that might want to eat it.

SEAWEED FARMS AREN'T ALWAYS GOOD!

Seaweed farms do have some negatives. For example, they reduce the amount of sunlight that reaches the seafloor. This makes it harder for things like seagrass to grow.

IT HAS BEEN USED FOR HEALTH PURPOSES FOR THOUSANDS OF YEARS!

The Ancient Greeks and Romans used seaweed to treat illnesses like coughs and colds. Today, it is often used as an ingredient in things like shampoo and soap, as well as in plasters and bandages.

GLOSSARY

Algae – a group of plant-like organisms that mostly grow in water. *Need help saying this? Look below!*

Carbon dioxide – an invisible gas in the air that plants take in to make food and oxygen (see right).

Chemicals – substances made up of the same tiny building blocks.

Climate change – a change in the weather conditions over a long time.

Coastline – the area where the land meets the sea.

Ecosystems – all the living and non-living things that exist together within an area.

Environment – everything that is around us.

Erosion – the process of land being worn away by wind or water.

Food chain – the order in which different animals eat each other to survive.

Greenhouse gas – a type of invisible gas that raises the temperature of the planet.

Habitats – the places where animals and plants live.

Nutrients – substances or ingredients that plants and animals need to live and grow.

Oxygen – an invisible gas in the air that people and animals need to breathe.

Photosynthesis – how plants make food from sunlight, water, and carbon dioxide (see left).

Pollution – harmful materials that have been released into the environment (see left).

Predators – animals that hunt other animals for food.

Shields – to protect against something.

Species – a group of living things that share characteristics and features. For example, blue whales and beluga whales are different species.

Stipes – the stems of seaweed.

HOW DO I SAY?

Algae
AL-gee

Halimeda
HAL-ih-MEE-da

Phycologists
fy-KOH-luh-jists

Phycology
fy-KOH-luh-jee

THE BIG QUESTIONS ANSWERED

This is more than just a series of books; it is a complete resource. Accompanying each book is a variety of FREE material to engage curious kids with science.

www.thebigquestionsanswered.com

Use the QR code to visit the website, download free resources, and discover other books in the series.

On the website, find out incredible things about phycologists, including what they do, some of their greatest discoveries, and the people who have made a difference in this field of science.

The material is also available for home or classroom use, supporting all the information in this book.

Teachers' & Parents' Resources
With discussion prompts, questions, and extra information around key topics.

Activity Pack
Fun activities including creative writing, word searches, and more.

Audio Book
Experience this book in audio, narrated by a professional voice actor.

The Big Questions Answered is published by Beetle Books. Beetle Books is an imprint of Hungry Tomato Ltd.

First published in 2025 by Hungry Tomato Ltd
F15, Old Bakery Studios, Blewetts Wharf, Malpas Road, Truro, Cornwall, TR1 1QH, UK.

ISBN 9781835691557

A CIP catalog record for this book is available from the British Library.

With thanks to:
Editors: Jenny Rowan and Holly Thornton
Designers: Meg Holbrook and Amy Harvey
The team at Beehive Illustration
Consultant: Kerry Holbrook

Information in this book is up to date as of the time of writing.

Printed and bound in China.

Picture Credits:
(t = top, b = bottom, m = middle, l = left, r = right)
Shutterstock: Damsea 5mr; Divelvanov 6tl; Eo naya 6bl; gnomeandi 4br; Joe Belanger 3br; michel arnault 6mr; Nungning20 5bl; Svetlana Zhukova 4ml; SHINART 32ml; Wirestock Creators 4tr.